by Iain Gray

Lang**Syne**

PUBLISHING

WRITING *to* REMEMBER

LangSyne

PUBLISHING

WRITING *to* REMEMBER

79 Main Street, Newtongrange,
Midlothian EH22 4NA
Tel: 0131 344 0414
E-mail: info@lang-syne.co.uk
www.langsyneshop.co.uk

Design by Dorothy Meikle
Printed by Printwell Ltd
© Lang Syne Publishers Ltd 2022

ISBN 978-1-85217-606-8

Wright

MOTTOES include:
To live without a wish concealed,
Deserve,
Endure and hope,
Truth conquers,
A mind conscious of right.

CREST:
A silver leopard's face.

NAME variations include:
Right
Write
Wrighte

Chapter one:

The origins of popular surnames

by George Forbes and Iain Gray

If you don't know where you came from, you won't know where you're going is a frequently quoted observation and one that has a particular resonance today when there has been a marked upsurge in interest in genealogy, with increasing numbers of people curious to trace their family roots.

Main sources for genealogical research include census returns and official records of births, marriages and deaths – and the key to unlocking the detail they contain is obviously a family surname, one that has been 'inherited' and passed from generation to generation.

No matter our station in life, we all have a surname – but it was not until about the middle of the fourteenth century that the practice of being identified by a particular surname became commonly established throughout the British Isles.

Previous to this, it was normal for a person to be identified through the use of only a forename.

But as population gradually increased and there were many more people with the same forename, surnames were adopted to distinguish one person, or community, from another.

Many common English surnames are patronymic in origin, meaning they stem from the forename of one's father – with 'Johnson,' for example, indicating 'son of John.'

It was the Normans, in the wake of their eleventh century conquest of Anglo-Saxon England, a pivotal moment in the nation's history, who first brought surnames into usage – although it was a gradual process.

For the Normans, these were names initially based on the title of their estates, local villages and chateaux in France to distinguish and identify these landholdings.

Such grand descriptions also helped enhance the prestige of these warlords and generally glorify their lofty positions high above the humble serfs slaving away below in the pecking order who had only single names, often with Biblical connotations as in Pierre and Jacques.

The only descriptive distinctions among the peasantry concerned their occupations, like 'Pierre the swineherd' or 'Jacques the ferryman.'

Roots of surnames that came into usage in England not only included Norman-French, but also Old French, Old Norse, Old English, Middle English, German, Latin, Greek, Hebrew and the Gaelic languages of the Celts.

The Normans themselves were originally Vikings, or 'Northmen', who raided, colonised and eventually settled down around the French coastline.

They had sailed up the Seine in their long-boats in 900AD under their ferocious leader Rollo and ruled the roost in north eastern France before sailing over to conquer England in 1066 under Duke William of Normandy – better known to posterity as William the Conqueror, or King William I of England.

Granted lands in the newly-conquered England, some of their descendants later acquired territories in Wales, Scotland and Ireland – taking not only their own surnames, but also the practice of adopting a surname, with them.

But it was in England where Norman rule and custom first impacted, particularly in relation to the adoption of surnames.

This is reflected in the famous *Domesday Book*, a massive survey of much of England and Wales, ordered by William I, to determine who owned what, what it was worth and therefore how much they were liable to pay in taxes to the voracious Royal Exchequer.

Completed in 1086 and now held in the National Archives in Kew, London, 'Domesday' was an Old English word meaning 'Day of Judgement.'

This was because, in the words of one contemporary chronicler, "its decisions, like those of the Last Judgement, are unalterable."

It had been a requirement of all those English landholders – from the richest to the poorest – that they identify themselves for the purposes of the survey and for future reference by means of a surname.

This is why the *Domesday Book*, although written in Latin as was the practice for several centuries with both civic and ecclesiastical records, is an invaluable source for the early appearance of a wide range of English surnames.

Several of these names were coined in connection with occupations.

These include Baker and Smith, while Cooks, Chamberlains, Constables and Porters were to be found carrying out duties in large medieval households.

The church's influence can be found in names such as Bishop, Friar and Monk while the popular name of Bennett derives from the late fifth to mid-sixth century Saint Benedict, founder of the Benedictine order of monks.

The early medical profession is represented by Barber, while businessmen produced names that include Merchant and Sellers.

Down at the village watermill, the names that cropped up included Millar/Miller, Walker and Fuller, while other self-explanatory trades included Cooper, Tailor, Mason and Wright.

Even the scenery was utilised as in Moor, Hill, Wood and Forrest – while the hunt and the chase supplied names that include Hunter, Falconer, Fowler and Fox.

Colours are also a source of popular surnames, as in Black, Brown, Gray/Grey, Green and White, and would have denoted the colour of the clothing the person habitually wore or, apart from the obvious exception of 'Green', one's hair colouring or even complexion.

The surname Red developed into Reid, while

Blue was rare and no-one wanted to be associated with yellow.

Rather self-important individuals took surnames that include Goodman and Wiseman, while physical attributes crept into surnames such as Small and Little.

Many families proudly boast the heraldic device known as a Coat of Arms, as featured on our front cover.

The central motif of the Coat of Arms would originally have been what was borne on the shield of a warrior to distinguish himself from others on the battlefield.

Not featured on the Coat of Arms, but highlighted on page three, is the family motto and related crest – with the latter frequently different from the central motif.

Adding further variety to the rich cultural heritage that is represented by surnames is the appearance in recent times in lists of the 100 most common names found in England of ones that include Khan, Patel and Singh – names that have proud roots in the vast sub-continent of India.

Echoes of a far distant past can still be found in our surnames and they can be borne with pride in commemoration of our forebears.

Chapter two:

Fields of battle

Derived from the Old English 'wrytha', or 'wyrhtha', indicating 'work', 'Wright' is a surname that originally denoted someone who made things, or 'wrought' – such as a wheelwright who made wheels, a shipwright who made ships, or a carpenter or anyone else who 'worked' with wood in general.

In common with many other names, it became popularised as a surname in the wake of the Norman Conquest of 1066 – although the ancestors of those who would come to bear it were present in England for a considerable period before this date.

This means that flowing through the veins of many Wrights today may well be the blood of those Germanic tribes who invaded and settled in the south and east of the island of Britain from about the early fifth century.

Known as the Anglo-Saxons, they were composed of the Jutes, from the area of the Jutland Peninsula in modern Denmark, the Saxons from

Lower Saxony, in modern Germany and the Angles from the Angeln area of Germany.

It was the Angles who gave the name 'Engla land', or 'Aengla land' – better known as 'England.'

They held sway in what became England from approximately 550 to 1066, with the main kingdoms those of Sussex, Wessex, Northumbria, Mercia, Kent, East Anglia and Essex.

Whoever controlled the most powerful of these kingdoms was tacitly recognised as overall 'king' – one of the most noted being Alfred the Great, King of Wessex from 871 to 899.

It was during his reign that the famous *Anglo-Saxon Chronicle* was compiled – an invaluable source of Anglo-Saxon history – while Alfred was designated in early documents as *Rex Anglorum Saxonum*, King of the English Saxons.

Other important Anglo-Saxon works include the epic *Beowulf* and the seventh century *Caedmon's Hymn*.

Through the Anglo-Saxons, the language known as Old English developed, later transforming from the eleventh century into Middle English – sources from which many popular English surnames of today, such as Wright, derive.

The Anglo-Saxons meanwhile, had usurped the power of the indigenous Britons – who referred to them as 'Saeson' or 'Saxones.'

It is from this that the Scottish Gaelic term for 'English people' of 'Sasannach' derives, the Irish Gaelic 'Sasanach' and the Welsh 'Saeson.'

We learn from the *Anglo-Saxon Chronicle* how the religion of the early Anglo-Saxons was one that pre-dated the establishment of Christianity in the British Isles.

Known as a form of Germanic paganism, with roots in Old Norse religion, it shared much in common with the Druidic 'nature-worshipping' religion of the indigenous Britons.

It was in the closing years of the sixth century that Christianity began to take a hold in Britain, while by approximately 690 it had become the 'established' religion of Anglo-Saxon England.

In October of 1066, Harold II, the last of the Anglo-Saxon kings, was killed at the battle of Hastings, in East Sussex, after Duke William of Normandy arrived with a mighty invasion force.

William was declared King of England on December 25, and the complete subjugation of his Anglo-Saxon subjects followed.

Those Normans who had fought on his behalf were rewarded with the lands of Anglo-Saxons, many of whom sought exile abroad as mercenaries.

Within an astonishingly short space of time, Norman manners, customs and law were imposed on England – laying the basis for what subsequently became established 'English' custom and practice.

But beneath the surface, old Anglo-Saxon culture was not totally eradicated, with some aspects absorbed into those of the Normans, while faint echoes of the Anglo-Saxon past is still seen today in the form of popular surnames such as Wright.

Bearers of the name were to be found all over the British Isles – but the surname is particularly associated with what is now the modern-day Scottish Borders' county of Berwickshire.

This county, whose southern border is with the English county of Northumberland, was once part of a more extensive Scottish territorial holding that took in Berwick-upon-Tweed, that now lies in Northumberland.

This market town, situated only two and a half miles from the present day border between England and Scotland, changed hands at least twelve times over a course of approximately 400 years until finally coming under English control in 1482.

Originally founded as an Anglo-Saxon settlement, it was the scene in March of 1296 of one of the bloodiest episodes in Scotland's Wars of Independence against England.

This was when a 30,000-strong English army led by Edward I – known and feared as 'The Hammer of the Scots' – attacked the town and slaughtered an estimated 11,000 of its inhabitants, including women and children.

The bodies were so numerous to bury, according to one contemporary source, that many were unceremoniously thrown down wells or cast into the sea.

In later centuries, bearers of the name have gained a particular distinction on the battlefield, with no less than three being awarded the Victoria Cross (VC), the highest award for valour in the face of enemy action for British and Commonwealth forces.

Born in 1826 in Ballymena, Co. Antrim, Alexander Wright was an Irish recipient of the honour.

A private in the 77th (East Middlesex) Regiment of Foot during the Crimean War, at the siege of Sebastopol in March of 1855 he single-handedly repelled an enemy attack, while three weeks later he was instrumental, despite his wounds, in capturing an enemy trench; he survived the war and died in 1858.

It was during a British military campaign in Nigeria known as the Kano-Sokoto Expedition, that Brigadier General Wallace Wright, then a 28-year-old lieutenant in the 1st Battalion, The Queen's Royal West Surrey Regiment, won his VC.

This was in February of 1903 when, with only 44 men, he held off an enemy charge; later promoted to Brigadier General, he died in 1953.

Born in Brighton in 1883, Theodore Wright was a posthumous recipient of the VC during the First World War.

He had been a captain in the 57th Field Company, Corps of Royal Engineers when, in August of 1914 at Mons, in Belgium, he and a fellow officer braved heavy fire to connect up the electric leads to a demolition charge placed on a bridge.

He was killed only a few days later while helping a wounded man into shelter; his medal is displayed at the Royal Engineers Museum, Kent.

Across the Atlantic, Admiral Jerauld Wright was the highly decorated American naval officer who was born in 1898 in Amherst, Massachusetts.

Serving in both the European and Pacific theatres during the Second World War and recognised as an expert in naval gunnery, he later served, from 1954 to 1960, as Supreme Allied Commander (Atlantic) for NATO.

With nicknames that included "Old Iron Heels" and "El Supremo", he was also responsible during the Cold War for overseeing the reorganisation of the U.S. Navy's Atlantic fleet.

In retirement, he and the retired British Admiral Sir Nigel Henderson led the initiative for the restoration on the Arbigland estate, near Kirkbean, in Kirkcudbright, in the southwest of Scotland, of the cottage that was the eighteenth century birthplace of John Paul Jones, the Scot recognised as "Father of the American Navy."

Now fully restored and housing a museum, the cottage opened to the public two years before Admiral Wright's death in 1995.

Born in Edinburgh in 1979, Corporal Mark Wright was a posthumous recipient of the George Cross.

This was for his valour when, serving with the 3rd Battalion of the Parachute Regiment in Helmand Province, Afghanistan, he was killed in

September of 2006 after entering a minefield to rescue injured comrades.

It was in his honour that Mark Wright House, a dedicated centre for army personnel recovering from their injuries, was opened in his native Edinburgh in August of 2009.

Chapter three:

Taking to the skies

Away from the battlefield, Wrights have also gained distinction through a range of more peaceful pursuits.

Two of the most famous bearers of the name were the brothers Wilbur and Orville Wright, the pioneering American aviators who made the world's first controlled, powered and heavier-than-air human flight.

Wilbur, born in 1867 in Millville, Ohio, and Orville, born four years later in Dayton, Ohio, are said to have had their fascination with flying first aroused when, as young lads, their father gave them a present of a toy 'helicopter' based on a design by the French aeronautical pioneer Alphonse Rénaud.

Gifted with extraordinary mechanical skills, the brothers set up in business manufacturing and repairing everything from bicycles and motors to printing presses, and this was to stand them in good stead when they came to build their first flying machines.

This culminated on December 17, 1903, at

Kitty Hawk, North Carolina, when an aircraft made from machinery and other materials cobbled together in their workshop, took to the air.

In separate flights, one of twelve seconds duration, one of 59 seconds and at an altitude of approximately 10ft, they flew lengths of 120ft and 852 ft respectively.

The rudimentary machine was later perfected as the Wright Flyer I, and the brothers went on to invent aircraft controls that made fixed wing flight possible.

Wilbur died only nine years after the historic flights, while his brother died in 1948, by which time aviation had truly come of age.

Their original aeroplane, made of spruce and powered by a petrol engine, is now on display in the Smithsonian in Washington, along with a plaque that records how: 'By original scientific research the Wright brothers discovered the principles of human flight. As inventors, builders and flyers they further developed the aeroplane, taught man to fly and opened the era of aviation.'

Still looking to the skies and much further beyond, William Wright, born in 1871 in San Francisco, was the American astronomer who, as director from 1935 to 1942 of the Lick Observatory, became famous for his work on the velocity of stars in our galaxy.

A recipient of the 1938 Gold Medal of the Royal Astronomical Society, he died in 1959, while the moon crater 'Wright' is named in his honour.

One bearer of the Wright name whose legacy survives as part of the urban landscape of America is Frank Lloyd Wright, who was born in 1867 in Richland Center, Wisconsin.

A promoter of the 'organic' school of architecture, Wright, who died in 1959, has been recognised by the American Institute of Architects as 'the greatest American architect of all time.'

Architect of more than 500 structures that include his own summer home of Taliesin near Spring Green, Wisconsin, the house known as Fallingwater in the mountains of Penna on Bear Run Creek, New York's Guggenheim Museum, his 1904 Unity Temple in Oak Park, Illinois and the Frank Lloyd Wright Home and Studio, also in Oak Park, Wright was honoured on a U.S. postage stamp issued in 1966.

From urban America to the far flung and frozen reaches of Antarctica, Sir Charles Seymour Wright, also known as Silas Wright, born in 1887 in

Toronto, was one of the intrepid members of Captain Robert Scott's ill-fated Terra Nova expedition of 1910 to 1913.

The young Canadian physicist and glaciologist was a member of the original team that set off with Scott from base camp at Cape Evans with the aim of reaching the South Pole.

Wright was among a supporting party that Scott sent back to base. Several months later he was the first to spot the tent containing the frozen bodies of Scott, Henry Bowers and Edmund Wilson.

Enlisting with the British Army's Royal Engineers during the First World War, he developed the trench wireless, while during the Second World War he developed devices to detect magnetic mines; knighted in 1946 for his war service, he died in 1975.

One particularly enterprising bearer of the Wright name was William Henry Wright who, starting off his working life as a butcher's apprentice, ended as an immensely wealthy gold mine owner and the founder of what flourishes today as Canada's national newspaper.

Better known as Bill Wright, and born in 1876 in Sleaford, Lincolnshire he swapped the apron of a butcher's apprentice for British Army uniform in

1897, serving throughout the Boer War in South Africa.

Immigrating to Canada in 1907, he joined his sister and her husband Edward Hargreaves, who had settled in northern Ontario.

Wright worked for a time with his brother-in-law, a master butcher, before the pair decided to seek their fortune by prospecting for gold.

It was in the Kirkland Lake region of northern Ontario that, one memorable evening in July of 1911, Hargreaves became lost while hunting for rabbits for their evening meal.

He fired a rifle shot to attract his brother-in-law's attention, and it was while Wright was walking towards the sound that he stopped in his tracks after blundering into an outcrop of quartz.

Even in the fading light, he was able to spot flecks of gold. Confirming this when he and Hargreaves returned to the spot in the better light of the following morning, they subsequently staked a number of claims on the land over the following weeks.

But the claims had to be more carefully examined, and the partnership between the pair ended for a time when Hargreaves decided to return from the wilds of Kirkland Lake to support his wife.

Braving the harsh conditions on his own, Wright persisted in further exploration, and the area that he staked out eventually resulted in the three gold mines of Lakeshore, Sylvanite and Wright-Hargreaves – from which an astonishing 13.5 million ounces of gold were extracted over the years.

Despite the immense wealth the former butcher's apprentice and soldier had accrued only five years after his original discovery, and the fact that he was nearly 40 years of age, Wright insisted on enlisting as a private in the Canadian Army in 1916.

He served with distinction on the Western Front, turning down the opportunity of promotion several times.

Returning to his mining interests at the end of the First World War, he built up what became one of Canada's major mining companies.

In 1936, fifteen years before his death, he used part of his vast fortune to acquire the two Toronto newspapers *The Globe* and *The Mail and Empire* and, along with George McCullagh, merged them as *The Globe and Mail* – Canada's leading national newspaper of today.

Chapter four:

On the world stage

Proud bearers of the Wright name have also excelled in other pursuits that include entertainment, sport and the arts.

Best known for her role as Ginny Weasley in the *Harry Potter* series of films, **Bonnie Wright** is the English actress who was born in London in 1991.

It was after her brother, an avid fan of J.K. Rowling's series of *Harry Potter* books, told her that she reminded him of the character, that she successfully auditioned for the first film in the series, the 2001 *Harry Potter and the Philosopher's Stone*.

She has since appeared in all the other film adaptations of the book, including the 2010 *Harry Potter and the Deathly Hallows: Part I*, and the 2011 *Deathly Hallows: Part II*.

Although born in London, it was in the United States that **Ben Wright** made his name as an actor on radio, television and film.

Born in 1915, he later settled in America, where from 1949 to 1950 he was the voice of Sherlock Holmes in a popular radio series of the name and, from 1951 to 1952, as Inspector Peter Black in the *Pursuit* series.

Wright, who died in 1989, also appeared in films that include *The Sound of Music* and *My Fair Lady*, while he was also the narrator for the 1963 film *Cleopatra*.

Married to the American actor Rip Torn, **Amy Wright** is the actress born in Chicago in 1950 whose films include the 1995 *The Scarlet Letter*, while on television **Gillian Wright** is the British actress best known for her role as Jean Slater in the popular BBC soap *EastEnders*.

The actress, who was born Gillian Hambidge in 1959 in Carshalton, south London, was a recipient in 2006 of a Mental Health Media Award for her character portrayal in *EastEnders* of a bipolar disorder sufferer.

Behind the camera lens, **Herbert Wright**, born in 1947 in Columbas, Indiana and who died in 2005, was the science fiction writer and producer best known for his work on *Star Trek: The Next Generation*, while **Joe Wright** is the English film director, born in London in 1972, who won a 2003 BAFTA Award for Best Serial Drama for *Charles II: The Power and the Passion*.

Best known as the co-creator, along with

Jonathan Glassner, of the television series *Stargate SG-1*, **Brad Wright** is the Canadian television producer, screenwriter and actor who was born in Toronto in 1961, while in the heat of the kitchen **Clarissa Dickson Wright** was a British celebrity chef.

Born in 1947 in St John's Wood, London she was best known as having been one half, along with the late Jennifer Paterson, of the 1990's television food series *Two Fat Ladies*; she died in 2014.

Bearers of the Wright name have also excelled in the highly competitive world of sport.

On the tennis court, **Beals Wright** was the leading American player from Boston who was U.S. Singles Champion in 1905 and Doubles Champion in 1904, 1905 and 1906.

The player, who was born in 1879, was inducted into the International Tennis Hall of Fame five years before his death in 1961.

From tennis to the fields of European football, **Billy Wright** was the talented English centre half who was the first footballer in the world to earn 100 caps playing for his country, captaining the England team on no less than 90 occasions between 1946 and 1959.

Born in 1924 in Ironbridge, Shropshire he spent his entire playing career with Wolverhampton

Wanderers – from 1939 to 1959 – while he was inducted into the English Football Hall of Fame in 2002, eight years after his death.

Now a radio and television personality, **Ian Wright** is the former English footballer who played for teams that include Crystal Palace, Arsenal, Celtic and Burnley. The striker, born in London in 1963, earned 33 caps playing for his country between 1991 and 1998.

In American football, **Anthony Wright** is the retired quarterback, born in 1976 in Vanceboro, North Carolina, who played for teams that include the Pittsburgh Steelers and, from 2007 to 2008, the New York Giants.

His namesake, **Anthony Wright**, is the field hockey sweeper, born in 1984 in Vancouver, who was a member of the Canadian national team that took gold at the 2007 Pan American Games.

On the golf course, **Pamela Wright**, born in 1964, is the Scottish professional golfer who played on the ladies European Tour and was a member of the European Solheim Cup team in the early 1990s.

Bearers of the Wright name have also left their mark on the landscape in the form of notable civil engineering projects.

Known as "the Father of American Civil Engineering", **Benjamin Wright** was the American engineer, born in 1770 in Wethersfield, Connecticut who served as chief engineer of both the Erie and the Chesapeake and Ohio canals in the early decades of the nineteenth century.

Another leading civil engineer was **Horatio Wright**, who also served as a general with the Union Army during the American Civil War of 1861 to 1865.

After the war Wright, who was born in 1820 in Clinton, Massachusetts and who died in 1899, was responsible for projects that included completion of the Washington Monument and New York's Brooklyn Bridge; Fort Horatio Wright, on the eastern tip of New York's Fishers Island, is named in his honour.

In the creative world of art, **Andy Wright** is the Canadian multi-media artist, born in 1971, whose best known work is the stunning video installation *Blind Man's Bluff* and who has been nominated several times for Canada's prestigious Sobey Art Award.

In a different artistic genre, **David Wright**, born in 1912 and who died in 1967, was the British illustrator best known for his creation in 1956 of the *Daily Mail* newspaper's *Carol Day* cartoon strip, and for his series of illustrations for *The Sketch*.

Born in 1917, **Doug Wright** was the English-born Canadian cartoonist who created the famous and long-running Canadian newspaper comic strip *Doug Wright's Family*. The cartoonist, who died in 1983, is honoured through Canada's annual Doug Wright awards, established in 2005 to recognise Canadian cartoonists and graphic artists.

In the equally creative world of literature, Carolyn D. Wright, better known as **C.D. Wright**, is the contemporary American poet, born in 1949 in Mountain Home, Arkansas whose works include the 1986 *Further Adventures with You* and the 2009 *40 Watts*.

Born in 1985 in Pickwick Dam, Tennessee, **Charles Wright** is the American poet who won the 1998 Pulitzer Prize for Poetry for his *Black Zodiac*, while another Pulitzer Prize winner is **Doug Wright**, the American playwright and screenwriter, born in 1962 in Dallas, who won the 2004 Pulitzer Prize for Drama for his play *I Am My Own Wife*.

Winner of no less than three of Canada's major literary awards – the Giller Prize, the Trillium Book Award and the Governor General's Award – **Richard B. Wright** is the Canadian novelist born in 1937 in Ontario.

It was for his 2001 novel *Callan* that he won the awards, while other honours of which he is a recipient are membership of the Order of Canada and an Honorary Doctor of Letters from Trent University.

Born in 1939 in Saskatoon, Saskatchewan, Laurali Rose Wright, better known as **L.R. Wright**, was the best-selling Canadian writer of mystery novels whose final novel, *Menace*, was published in 2001, the year of her death.

A fashion model and photographer in addition to children's author, **Dare Wright**, born in 1914 in Thornhill, Ontario and later moving with her family to Cleveland, Ohio, was the author of books that include *The Lonely Doll* and *Edith and the Duckling*; she died in 2001.

From the world of the written word to the world of music, **Betty Wright**, born in 1953 in Miami, Florida is the Grammy Award-winning rhythm and blues and soul singer recognised as having influenced the development of the hip-hop genre.

Her 1975 single *Where is the Love* won a Grammy for best rhythm and blues song, while other hits include the 1989 *Keep Love New*.

Known as 'The Prince of the Blues', **Billy Wright**, born in 1932 in Atlanta and who died in

1991, was the American 'jump blues' artiste whose hits include the 1949 *Blues for My Baby* and the 1959 *Have Mercy, Baby*.

In contemporary music **Chely Wright**, born in Kansas City in 1970, is the country music singer who had a No. 1 American hit in 1999 with the single *White Female*.

Considered to have been one of the founders of the 'gangsta rap' genre, Eric Lynn Wright, born in 1963 in Compton, California and better known as **Eazy-E**, was the American rapper and record producer whose hit albums include the 1988 *Eazy-Duz-It*; he died in 1995.

Born in 1943 in Middlesex, **Richard Wright** was the songwriter, vocalist and keyboardist with the British progressive rock band Pink Floyd; he died in 2008.

Born in 1972 in Frankfurt, Germany, the son of an American helicopter pilot during the Vietnam War, Frank Edwin Wright III is the drummer for the American punk band Green Day better known by his rather more colourful stage name of **Tré Cool**.

One particularly controversial bearer of the Wright name was the British scientist and counter-intelligence officer **Peter Wright**.

Born in 1916 in Chesterfield, Derbyshire he served during the Second World War with the Admiralty Research Laboratory, and was later recruited as principal scientific officer for the British intelligence agency MI5.

It was shortly after his retirement from MI5 and subsequent move to Australia that, in 1985, his sensational and best-selling memoirs were published as *Spycatcher* – a book that the British authorities unsuccessfully fought through the courts to suppress on the grounds that it breached the Official Secrets Act.

The book made newspaper headlines around the world, with Wright's claims that not only had the agency he had worked for been involved in the illegal planting of listening devices, or 'bugs', but also that a secret group within MI5 had been involved in a plot in the 1970s to remove the then Labour Prime Minister Harold Wilson from power.

Wright, who also controversially claimed that the former Soviet intelligence agency the KGB had infiltrated a number of British institutions, including MI5 itself, died in 1995.